Only a Dog

A Story of the Great War

By Bertha Whitridge Smith

First Published in 1917 by E. P. Dutton & Co.

681 Fifth Avenue, NY, USA

This illustrated edition published 2025 by Cosmic Jive Publishing

ISBN 978-1-918219-40-1

Bespoke illustrations and also compilation and editing of other licensed artwork by Jack Champion, 2025

To

THOSE DEVOTED AMERICANS
WHO ARE GIVING THEIR LIVES
TO THE RELIEF OF SUFFERING IN EUROPE.
THEY ARE DWELLING ON THE HILL-TOPS,
AND IT WILL BE THEIR PRIVILEGE
TO SEE THE FIRST GLOW OF THE
DAWN OF A NEW WORLD CONSCIENCE

AUTHOR'S NOTE

This story of the bravery of a man, the faithfulness of a dog, the kind heart of the British Tommy, and the wanton cruelty of the German "Hun," is quite true, and was given to me by Major Edgar, R. A. M. C. (of Montreal) with his kind permission to elaborate it into its present form.

It all happened near Armentieres in Flanders, and it is there, that anyone who cares to look, may find the big grave with the little one beside it, both marked by the same cross, and on it, the legend:

NO. 678962 — PRIVATE RICE AND "ARMY"

Bertha Whitridge Smith

Whatever money comes from the sale of this little book will be used for materials to make dressings for the wounded soldiers of the Allies, and it is perhaps not too much to hope that little Army's life-story may be the means of easing the suffering of many brave soldiers like "P'te. Rice."

B. W. S.

BISHOP DOANE ON HIS DOG

*I am quite sure he thinks that I am God —
Since He is God on whom each one depends
For life, and all things that His bounty sends —
My dear old dog, most constant of all friends;
Not too quick to mind, but quicker far than I
To Him whom God I know and own: his eye,
Deep brown and liquid, watches for my nod;
He is more patient underneath the rod
Than I, when God His wise corrections sends.
He looks love at me, deep as words e'er spake:
And from me never crumb nor sup will take
But he wags thanks with his most vocal tail:
And when some crashing noise wakes all his
fear, He is content and quiet if I am near,
Secure that my protection will prevail.
So, faithful, mindful, thankful, trustful, he
Tells me what I unto my God should be.*

Only a Dog

A Story of the Great War

I

"There is a world outside the one you know."
— KIPLING.

AS I lie here on my dear Master's breast, waiting for him to wake, I have much time to think of all that has happened to me, and through the many long days, and weary dark cold nights, I try to make the time seem shorter by talking it all out to myself.

I have sometimes heard People say, "He's only a dog, never mind about him," and I do wonder why they speak so, because really it seems to me that we are wiser than they are.

It is true we cannot speak their language any more than they can ours, but we do understand almost everything they say, and try as we may, we cannot make them understand us, except the very easy things about being tired or hungry, or something like that.

Once in a while, we do find someone like my dear Master lying here, who talks to us just as if he knew we had real deep thoughts and could appreciate his. However, all this is neither here nor there until I have told my story.

I was born in a most beautiful place, the "Chateau de T— " they called it, and unlike many little dogs, I was allowed to stay long enough with my Mother to learn how to behave, and how to take many things in the world, which often trouble us young ones very much indeed. She used to say, "You must always remember, my child, that People have the power to make your life happy or miserable, and that if you always try to behave well, and do what you are told, you will generally be well treated.

"Of course, there are some cruel men who take pleasure in tormenting us, and when you meet that kind, you will be justified in using all the means of defence that Nature gave you. You have very sharp claws and still sharper teeth, and will generally be able to make People very much afraid of you, if you use them.

"But when you find a good kind master, be obedient to him, and faithful to the death."

Another thing she told me, was, that although I had been born in France, I was really an Irishman, and could hold up my tail with the best-bred poodle in this country, and that I must never allow myself to be overawed by any of their grand airs, but let them know that I had the finest forbears a dog could have.

I have always been very glad she told me this, because when I have seen one of those poodles with carved hair and waxed mustaches, looking like a bloomin' Punch and Judy show, come tiptoeing towards me, I have felt sure that it was all right for me to tiptoe up to him, with the same air of insolence, and to give him what- for.

When I left my Mother, I went to live in a much smaller house than the Chateau, but quite near by, so that I was often taken to see her.

I lived with two very nice kind children, a boy and a girl, and they took me with them wherever they went, even if it were as far as Paris or London, so that I saw a great deal of the world.

We had been very happy together for a

number of years, when there came a hot morning in midsummer and all of us in he breakfast room together. All at once, I heard my oldest Master make a loud exclamation; something about "War" having come at last, and that his uniform must be got ready as he would have to go to Paris immediately to join his regiment.

I did not quite understand what all this meant, so I was pleased when my youngest Master called out, "Mon Pere, what do you mean by your uniform?' and to hear his Father say, "My soldier clothes, little Jean. Papa has to go to war and be a soldier."

My little Master and I both knew from the anxious looks of the family, that this must be something very sad and sorrowful, and when we went out to the garden together, he threw himself on the ground and putting his arms around me cried, "Oh! boy! my dear Irish boy! I am afraid my Papa will be killed!"

I licked him and nuzzled him all I could to show my sympathy, and I did seem to be a comfort to him.

After this, things began to happen very quickly, and hardly had the oldest Master gone, than soldiers began to come to the house. Every time they came, they took something away with them. The day they took the horses from the stable, Jean and I stood watching them, and suddenly he turned to me and said, "Oh! my boy! they might want to take you too! Run! Run quickly, and hide!" pointing to a place in the shrubbery.

I felt very rebellious at this, for it looked

too much like being a coward to suit me, so I only looked at him and did not move. But when he stamped his foot angrily, and said, "Go!" in a loud voice, I thought best to humour him and turned to obey.

Just as I did so, one of the soldiers noticed me, and called to his officer to ask if he should take me. Now, I did not at all want to go away with those strange men, even though they were taking my friends from the stable, so I just laid myself down at my little Master's feet, hoping they would see that I could not leave him.

The officer took a good look at me, and another at little Jean, and then I was much relieved to hear him say, "No, we will not take him, I think the child needs him more than we do; though he looks a good sort."

After this day, we soon began to hear sounds like thunder in the distance, and as I never did like thunder I was glad enough to stay inside the house, especially as the queerest kind of procession began to go by. Men, women, and children, cows, pigs, old lame horses, and often dogs and cats, and once in a while birds, carried in open boxes;

and everybody hung all over with bundles or babies. Even the children, and the dogs, had almost more than they could carry, and many of them dragged heavily loaded little carts as well.

As we sat in the window and watched all these things, I did long to ask my youngest Master what it all meant, but of course it wasn't any use to try, even if he had been able to explain, and so I made up my mind to listen to everything I could hear. In this way, I learned that the War had begun in earnest, and was coming closer and closer to us, and that all these people we saw were leaving their nice comfortable homes, because they were afraid of the "Germans."

I did wonder what a "German" was, so I kept my ears wide open, and when one day Marie, the cook, came running to my oldest

Mistress calling out, "Madame! Madame! The Germans!" I flew out into the garden to see for myself.

Rushing to the gate which stood open, I looked down the road, and saw away off in the distance a big cloud of dust, and as I kept on looking very hard, I presently made out big black horses, with big men on them, who wore queer shining pointed caps on their heads.

I was so excited, I trembled all over from head to foot, but I did not feel afraid, and remembered to hold my tail well up in case they should be like those impudent poodles.

When they came up to me, partly because I was so excited and partly because I felt unaccountably savage, I bared my teeth, and gave the deepest growl I knew how, and this must have made them angry, for the head one leaned over the side of his horse and hit me so hard with a kind of gleaming stick he carried in his hand, the blood ran, and I was rolled over and over on the ground.

I should have been trampled to death under the horses' feet, if I hadn't jumped up very quickly, and dashed back through the gate to the house, where my oldest Mistress, who was standing at the door, caught me in her arms.

They stopped at the gate, those "Germans" and the head one called out in the roughest voice I ever heard, that ten of them would eat and sleep, and to get ready!

I did wonder how my oldest Mistress could answer them as sweetly as she did, but she welcomed them and gave them everything they wanted.

Late that night, they seemed to be making a great deal of noise, and I thought I heard women's voices screaming, but as I had been shut up in the tool-house outside in the garden, I could not be sure; and when, after a long, long time, the noises stopped, I fell asleep.

II

"Smells are surer than sounds or sights
To make your heart-strings crack —
They start those awful voices o 'nights
That whisper, "Old Man, come back!"
— KIPLING.

WHEN I awoke, I could see out of the high window that the sun was shining, and I wanted very much to get out of the tool-house. I whined and whined, hoping somebody would hear me, and I was very sure that if my youngest Master could hear me, he at least would understand, but nobody came

and it was so silent, I grew more and more miserable, and being very hungry and frightened, I barked finally, just as loud as I could.

If there was any one to hear, they certainly did not understand, for nobody came to help me, and after a while when I was quite tired out with barking and scratching, I lay down to think what was best to be done.

I suppose I slept again, for when I noticed once more, I could see from the look of the sunshine that it must be quite late in the day, and the only sound I could hear, though I listened with my ears at their very highest, was the humming of the bees around their hives in the garden.

I looked around me carefully for some way of escape, and noticing on the door the piece of iron which fastened it, and remembering that my little Master used to lift it when he wanted to get out, I wondered if I couldn't push it up with my nose.

It was very high above my head, but as it seemed the only way, I determined to try, so again and again I jumped, and jumped, without the least success. I did not despair, however, but just decided to take a rest and then to gather all my strength for one big leap, so lifting my legs under me and as near under the iron piece as I could, I made one grand effort and wonder of wonders! succeeded.

The door opened a small crack and to push it wide was easy, but I did it slowly and with great caution, for I was filled with an anxiety and dread I could not understand, and put my head out to look around before I ventured any more.

I could see that the garden was all trampled, but no one seemed to be near, so I came out slowly and smelled about, and found that horses and men both had been trampling the grass my oldest Mistress was so fond of, and had broken all the lovely flowers.

As I still saw no signs of People, and was very hungry and still more thirsty, I crept slowly to the house where the door hung wide open, and just inside, as usual my bowl, with only a few drops of water. I lapped these eagerly; then feeling better, took courage to seek further for my little Master or some of the family.

Still creeping silently, though I did not quite know why, I went through the hall where things seemed to be much as usual, and then to the breakfast room where there was the most dreadful mess over everything, of plates, and food, and broken china, and glass.

Hungry and worried as I was, I could not

help wondering how it was that my careful oldest Mistress could have left the place in such a condition.

I tried to eat some pieces of food I found on the floor, but everything had a very odd taste, and such a strong smell it made me sneeze and feel quite sick, so I went on from room to room, still seeing no one and unable to smell any of my dear People,

Only A Dog

because of that horrid sickening stuff, whatever it was.

At last I came to the little room where I had been accustomed to stay so much with my youngest Master, and to lie and sleep before the fire while he amused himself.

As I crept across the floor, I saw that somebody was lying on the couch at the other side, but I could not quite tell whether it was my oldest Mistress, or Marie the cook; and just then, my foot touched something wet on the floor. I put down my nose to smell, and quickly realized that it was blood I had stepped into!

Now blood had always seemed to me a very delicious kind of food, particularly the fresh blood of a nice young chicken when once in a while I had managed to steal off by myself and kill one, but somehow, this did not tempt me at all. It had a most peculiar smell and I felt quite sickened again, so I drew back and tried to get to the couch another way, and finally got so near that by stretching out my neck, I could touch a hand, which hung down almost to the floor.

The light was too dim to see clearly, but I knew it was a hand, and on it there was again that dreadful blood I could not bear to taste, so I reached a little further and nuzzled at the arm, and made sure it was my oldest Mistress lying there, though in spite of whines and scratches, and little barks, I could not make her speak.

I waited, and waited, until it grew quite dark and there was not a sound, — not in the room, nor in the whole house, nor outside, — and I began to tremble and to get more frightened, until at last I felt I could not bear it another second, and I crept out of the room, trying not to touch that dreadful blood.

I knew that it was my work to look further for my little Master, and to search upstairs where he might be needing me, so gathering my courage as best I could, I went fearfully up the stairs and from room to room, finding not a sign of any that I loved and only dirt and disorder, and the beds all flung about.

After searching everywhere, I gave it up and pattered down again, and as I passed the door of the little room, an unaccountable terror seized me. I felt my hair rising all along my back, and then there seemed to be Something, or Somebody, I could not see, and I flew through the hall, and out the big door, bumping against things but not minding; through the garden, and out through the open gate to the road.

Down the road I ran — and ran — and ran — and ran, and the faster I went, the faster the terror seemed to come after me.

As I look back, it seems to me that I ran the whole night through, but I suppose I must have stopped to breathe sometimes, and all the time, I never met a soul, because if I came near anything I thought might be human I turned another way, or crept into a bush.

All the sadness and trouble had come since I had heard so much about "Germans," and my own experiences had taught me already that I could not give them too wide a berth, for good fighter as I knew myself to be, I was powerless among them.

At last, I was so exhausted I felt I could run no more, and as the day had begun to dawn and to light up the black darkness, I felt less afraid, and determined to lie down and rest if I could only find a place where I might feel safe.

In the distance, I could see the outlines of houses, and knew there must be a village, but I did not want to go near it until it was bright day, when I could perhaps tell something about the People, whether they were friends, or that terrible enemy. So I ran into a thick lot of trees and bushes near by.

After scratching a bed together as best I

could, I lay down without much fuss of turning and choosing, being too utterly tired out to care, and shutting my eyes, I tried to think a little about what I should do to find my dear family.

III

*" Towns without people, ten times took,
An' ten times left an' burned at last!
An' starvin' dogs that came to look
For owners, when a column passed — "*
— KIPLING.

I DID not succeed in doing much thinking, because as soon as I closed my eyes, I saw that dreadful room again, and my poor oldest Mistress lying there on the couch! Then I tried to keep my eyes open, but I could not, and in spite of the horrors and fears, I fell asleep.

It seemed only a moment, but must have been a good long time, because when I came to myself, the sun was shining quite high up in the sky, and feeling very sore and tired still, I crept out of the bushes into the warmth of the sunshine and sat down to think what I should do.

I was very hungry and quickly decided that the first thing was to find something to eat, and that unless there was something to hunt in the wood where I had slept, I must try to find some kind People in those houses, which looked nearer in the daylight.

It did not take me long to discover that there were only birds in the wood, and though I had sometimes caught them, it was no use to try now when I felt so sore and lame, so I crept cautiously towards the houses, keeping under bushes, in case I saw a "German." As no one seemed to be about, however, my courage began to rise and I trotted along a little faster, until I came to a house which stood a little way out of the village by itself, and I went around it carefully to see what I could find.

Just as I had nearly given up hope of finding anything, I saw the door of the

house open, a little crack at first, and then wide enough for a queer-looking old woman to put her head out.

She looked about her just the way I had done when I got out of the tool-house, so I could understand just how she was feeling, and I wondered if she had been frightened by the "Germans" too. At any rate, I did not feel at all afraid of her, and as she came out of the door, I walked up to her wagging my tail, and trying in every possible way to make her see what I wanted.

She looked at me in an odd sort of way, and I heard her whisper, "Pauvre chien — pauvre chien." Then she bent down and tried to brush some of the dirt off me, but though I knew I must be a sight, what I wanted most was food and drink.

I looked very hard in her face and whined the little low whine which means distress, hoping she would understand, but she did not seem to, so I pushed past her into the house. I went smelling about everywhere until I found a cupboard, with half-open door, where on a low shelf there was a large piece of bread and a piece of bone, which I could easily reach, though I did not know if I might have it.

As the woman did not come in after me, I thought she couldn't care much, so I snatched the bread and gulped it down in great pieces which nearly choked me, and when I had finished it, I took the bone and went out of the door, where the woman was still standing just as I had left her.

She did not seem to see me, so I lay down near her and began to gnaw the bits of meat, and as I worried over the bone, I watched her, and saw her draw her hand across her eyes several times as if she were trying to wake. Then I heard her say again, in the same odd whisper, "Pauvre, pauvre chien! Art thou too, like me, terrified and alone? Hast thou heard sounds and seen sights to madden thee? Are all thy dear ones gone too, and thyself better dead, as they are?"

Only A Dog

All the time I worked over the bone, she stood there just the same, whispering once in a while, and sometimes, I caught a word or two, like "Jtsu," and "Pittt."

When I had quite finished and had found a drink from some water in the yard, I went over to her and rubbed myself against her, and licked her hand, and pulled at her skirt, but she never noticed me more than to pat my head a little, so at last I gave it up, for though I felt very grateful to her for the food and very sorry for her, she did not belong to me, and I knew I must hurry on.

I went away slowly, looking back now and again, hoping she would call me, but she just stood there quite still, and I could see she was not thinking of me, at all.

From there, I went on through the village

and was astonished to find that the houses were only broken walls, and that inside were only heaps of stones and broken things, and not a Person anywhere.

I went on and on from house to house noticing that some were blackened by fire, and others just knocked down, as I had often seen my youngest Master knock down his block houses, and when I had got quite to the other end, I was rejoiced to see another dog.

I ran up to him, and though at first he was not friendly, when I talked to him and told him all I had been through and how completely I was lost, he became very willing to talk to me.

I asked all about the village and whether he had lived here before, and when I found he had, I thought he might know whether it was anywhere near the Chateau de T —, which was the place where I thought I might possibly find some of my dear People, if only I could learn the way.

He did not know and, like the old woman, did not seem to mind very much about anything. He refused to come with me, because, he said, he must stay by what had been his home, in case any of his People came back.

I asked him if it was "Germans" who had done all this to his village, but he was evidently not educated, for he did not seem to understand, and just laid himself down quite hopelessly on a very uncomfortable pile of stones in his house, so I said I must run on.

IV

"Rivers at night that cluck an' jeer,
Plains which the moonshine turns to sea,
Mountains which never let you near.
An' stars to all eternity —"
— KIPLING.

I TROTTED up and down about the country all that day, without ever coming to the Chateau or any place that looked at all familiar, and I spent the night as before under some bushes.

When morning came again, I found I was in quite an open country with no houses anywhere that I could see, and chasing about after food, I was fortunate enough to catch a couple of field-mice which I ate bones and all, though I had never deigned to eat such food before.

Finding a nice clear brook, I had a good long drink, and then I laid down in the water and had a good soak, for it was the first time I had been able even to try to clean myself since I had been rolled under the hoofs of that big black horse, by that dreadful shining stick.

As the country seemed so open, I decided to go up to the top of a high hill I saw in the distance, thinking that from there I might see the towers of the Chateau de T— . I trotted along in the hot sun for hours without the hill appearing to be much nearer, and got quite discouraged, for I hadn't dreamed it would be so far. But I never was one to give up easily, and so I trotted on, and on, and late in the afternoon found myself at last, at the very top.

When I looked over the other side of the hill, there was no sign of anything like the Chateau as I had hoped, but far off in the distance I saw what I thought must be a town, and still beyond that a river, winding at the foot of hills much higher than the one I was on.

I sat down to rest, and to look, and consider what I should do. If I stayed out in a place like this by myself I should certainly starve before long, and not be able to find any of my dear People, so I thought I had better try to get to the town where perhaps some Person might be kind to me, and where if I listened carefully to all that People said, I might hear something about what had happened to my little Master.

I went down the hill as fast as I could, for I knew that if I did not find the town before the dark came, I should lose my way and perhaps never find it; just the same as I lost my own house, because I ran away in such a fright in the night and never looked where I was going.

When I got to the bottom of the hill, and found myself all alone in the open, with not even a bush to give me cover, I did feel nervous, but it was no use to give way to that, besides, so far as I could see there was not a Person anywhere. Indeed, I could not even see any animals either, and it did seem strange when I came to think about it that I had seen so few animals anywhere I had been. It made me feel that there must be something very wrong somewhere, if even the little beasts in the fields had to hide or fly for their lives. When I had begun to think about this, I got more worried than ever, and stopped to look around me once more.

There was still the town in front of me,

and off to one side from that, the river and the mountains, just as I had seen them from the hill-top. Between me and the town, there was a long flat plain which seemed to be all dust and dirt, and just two ridges, not very high; they hardly looked higher to me than the ridges the men make in the fields when they plough. But these were very far apart.

I decided after a bit that I would go right down the middle of that ground between the ridges, as it seemed my straightest way to the town; so I pulled myself together once more, and remembered to keep my tail well up and my head too so that I could see, and with my ears pricked high for listening. I trotted on as bravely as I could.

I know now only too well that the path I had chosen was the deadly "No Man's

Land" which lay between the British and the German trenches, and that my nervous fears had a firmer foundation than I dreamed; but I have heard People say that "Ignorance is bliss," and it was like that with me, so on I went.

The sun at this time was nearly down to the tops of the hills, and as it was shining directly in my eyes, it was very hard for me to see. I was thinking how glad I should be when it was gone, when I heard nice kind English voices coming faintly from I knew not where, and then a louder whistling call, which I understood very well as an invitation, so I turned to run to the place from which I thought it sounded.

As I turned, I heard a whizzing something come from behind me and rush through the air just above my head, and then another, and another, and then laughter, which seemed to be quite far away and also behind me. My eyes were too blinded by the sun to see, even if I had dared to stop and look, so I tried to run even faster towards the kind whistling voices, which were louder and kinder than before, when I was suddenly knocked off my feet, and rolled over, by a terrible blow which took my breath away.

When I came to myself, the sun was gone and it was fast growing dusk, but remembering the friendly voices, I tried to get on my legs again, and was dismayed to find after many attempts, that all I could do was to sit up a very little, as my hind legs were quite useless and the blood running from them.

For a minute after this, I lost my courage

entirely and, lifting up my head, I uttered one long howl of despair, but only one, for as soon as I had done this, there came more of those whizzing things falling near me, so I lay down again and kept very quiet, hoping it would soon be dark, and that I could die in peace, if die I must.

Just as I had made up my mind to this, I heard from in front of me a dear kind English voice, calling in a whisper, "Come, boy! Come!" but alas! I could not come, which the owner of the voice seemed to understand, for he kept on whispering kind encouraging words, and they sounded nearer and nearer, until, at last, I saw in the dim light that a man, the colour of the earth itself, was coming towards me, crawling and wriggling on the ground the way snakes come, and as soon as he was near enough, he took me very carefully in his arms.

"Poor little laddie!" he said softly, "did those d — d beastly 'Uns try ter shoot yer? They shan't 'urt yer any more, if Rice P-t-e- can 'elp," and with that, he had got me somehow on his shoulders, and was squirming back the way he came.

I did suffer dreadfully, but determined not to make any sound, for I had already learned that if I did, there would be more of those bullets (as I afterwards knew they were called) coming after us; and, as it was, I have never understood how we got through safely. When we got to the edge of what had looked to me like a ridge, more kind voices called out, quite loud this time, "Well done, Rice! well done, old man!" and reaching out strong hands, they caught him and me together, and pulled us down inside.

Bertha Whitridge Smith

It was almost dark in that place, but I could just see that there were many men, and heard them ask somebody if they might give "them" what-for ! Then a second after, there was the loudest sound I ever heard in my life, and I knew no more.

V

"An quiet 'omesick talks between —
Men, met by night, you never knew
Until —'is face — by shell fire seen —,
Once — an' struck off. *They* taught me too"
— KIPLING.

WHEN I again became conscious of what was going on around me, I felt that my hind legs were all wrapped up so that I could not even try to move them, and I was lying somewhere in the dark, alone. There was nothing I could do, so I had to wait as patiently as I could, and it was not so very long, for presently I heard men's voices and saw a faint light.

One of the men came and looked at me and seeing that my eyes were open, he smoothed my head gently, and I heard him say to the others, "I've got permission ter carry the dog back ter the 'Orspital. I'll find somebody to 'elp me with 'im."

"Sure enough ye will, an' I'll go along ter tell the story ter the Surgeon, fer ye'll niver lat 'im know it all yerself, if I knows ye, Jack Rice," said another.

The first man, the one they called Rice, whom I knew at once to be the kind friend who had saved me at the risk of his own life, picked me up as gently as he could, and though it hurt me terribly, I licked his hand to show that I was grateful, for wag my tail

I could not.

He carried me out into the night, all the time whispering in my ear, "Poor little laddie, no need ter be frightened, ye're with friends now." And then I heard him say to his pal: "The poor little bloke's just skin an' bones. I'll bet 'e's 'ad a good long run from somew'eres."

As we went what seemed to me a long, long way, I could see stars shining above; and all along by the roadside the shadows of big wagons, and of horses standing about, and I supposed this must be the "army" I had heard my oldest Master talk about, that time, now so far away, before he left home to join it.

Before long, we came to a bright light in front of a fine big house which appeared to be in the midst of many other houses, and on the door, I saw a white cloth hanging, with red marks across it. I had never seen such a thing before, but now of course I know that it was the sign of the Red Cross, to show everybody that it is the place where they can find help and comfort.

We went in, and I could see Rice trying, with difficulty, having me in his arms, to touch his cap to somebody who asked what he wanted, and I heard him say that he had brought a poor homeless dog wounded by the Germans, and he wanted the Surgeon to see if he couldn't do something for him.

We waited some time, and then we went into a room where everybody had the oddest looking white clothes on, and I heard Rice's friend telling all about how he and Rice were "snipers" and had seen me coming down through "No Man's Land" from their lookout, and how, "He cum a trottin' along jist the same's ef he'd bin in Hyde Park, his head an' tail up jist as sassy as yer please"; and then all the rest of the story.

Before he finished, they had taken me from Rice and put me on a table, though he stood close to me and kept his hand on me.

Then they gave me something very nasty to smell, and I struggled as hard as I could, but had to give in at last feeling very miserable indeed. My only comfort, the thought that this kind man, who had done so much for me, would surely not let anybody harm me now.

After what seemed only a few minutes, I heard a strange voice say, "There, my man, I have done all I can, and my very best, in spite of it's being only a dog, and glad to do it for the brave fellow you have shown yourself to be."

There it was again, "only a dog," and feeling quite cross with the Surgeon, I showed my teeth when he put his hand on me and determined that I would certainly try to do something if I lived, to show People that they really were the ones who had not proper understanding. However, he had at least praised my kind friend, and for that I was grateful, so I listened quietly while he explained that he thought if I were kept very quiet, and well looked after, I might get well, and that I could be left there if Rice wished.

You can imagine how delighted I was to hear my friend say he thought it would be best to take me back with him, where he could look after me himself.

When we got back, it was beginning to be light, and I could see that we went down into the earth where there were quite nice rooms dug out, and I was made comfortable on a sort of bed in the corner of one of them.

As the days went by, everybody tried to

do something for me, and the men would come and bring me things to eat, until Rice said, "'E'll be dead spoilt, the little beggar." They all had something to say too about what I should be called, for after they had tried every name they could think of and I would not answer, they said I must have a new name.

They suggested all kinds of names which did not interest me at all, and at last my dear Master said I should be called "Army," because I belonged to it; and that made me feel very proud.

Of course, I was often alone while I was too ill to move, and had a great deal of time to think. I felt very sorry that I had never found my little Master Jean nor any of his dear People, but I could not see that it was my fault, and I realized that I never again should be able to travel about the country looking for them, so it was best to put them out of my mind, and to take this good kind friend for my Master.

The time I came to this conclusion was one morning when my dear Master was getting ready to go out to his sniping post, and feeling for the first time that I could move a little, I crawled off the bed and dragged myself to where he stood and laid myself down at his feet. He seemed very delighted and began to talk to me just as if he understood perfectly how I felt.

He did understand, for he said, Oh! so kindly, "Yes, boy, I know ye're grateful, and so am I, for I used ter be so lonely, an' now ye're gettin' well, we'll be chums tergether 'allus, won't we?" I licked his hand and did my best, weak as I was, to show my joy, and then he put me back on my bed and went out.

After this, began the very happiest time of my life, for although I never got well enough to run hard as before, I was able to trot about after my dear Master, and am glad to think I never left him day or night.

Only A Dog

Most of the men had to sleep in the daytime, and work at night, but my Master, because he was a "sniper," had to sit or stand all day looking out for the enemy; and every now and then shooting.

I stayed always with him, and he talked to me constantly, and always told me what he saw and whether he had hit anyone. Once I got so excited when he was particularly pleased, I jumped about and barked out loud, but I never did it again, for in a second, the bullets began to come around us and my Master had to crouch down on the ground with me for safety.

He was never angry, but he spoke very seriously to me about this, and said: "Army must never do such a thing again, because it shows the h'enemy jus' w'ere the lookout is."

There were days when everything was quiet, and it seemed hardly worth while for us to keep such close watch. Then, my Master would say, "It's dull, Army, me boy, but I'll just keep watchin' an' maybe I'll get a shot at Fritzie w'en 'e ain't a thinkin' "; and there were other days when there would be the most frightful noises, and he would say, "Fritzie's puttin' over some 'eavy stuff terday, boy; it's gettin' a bit too close fer my taste." But whatever came, he was always at his post, and I with him.

At night when he slept, I kept a close watch for the rats, so that he should not be disturbed, and before long, I had killed so many of them, they passed the word along among themselves and dared not come within earshot of me.

Sometimes at night too there was

terrible fighting, and one night, my Master never went to bed at all, and he told me that they were going to make a big "push" and that when the word came for the men to dash out, I had better stay behind, for he might be killed, and I might too, and that I couldn't do any good.

I listened to him and made no answer. of course, but privately. I determined that I should go wherever he went, for if he had to be killed, I certainly did not want to live without him, and I might be a help somehow.

We watched and waited a long time, and the thundering guns made a horrible din, and the shells screeched through the air "like lost souls" my Master said, and then suddenly I heard a loud voice call "Forward!" and "Come on! get on! you blitherers! Let 'em have steel! curse 'em!"

We dashed outside the trench with all the others, and found it was just beginning to be a little light in the sky, and we could just see the enemy rushing towards us, as we ran towards them, all of us meaning death and destruction, just as hard as ever we could. It was horrible the way the men killed, and killed, and killed, and I was glad enough to keep always at my Master's heels, and when he struggled with a "Hun" I helped all I could, and bit, and scratched.

At last, after it had gone on a long time, a big "German" (I knew him by his pointed cap) got my Master down, and just as he lifted his arm with a big gleaming knife to kill him, I jumped and caught him by the throat, and he was so astonished, besides being weak from loss of blood, I suppose, I was able to shake him to death just as I did a rat. My Master lay quite still and I was afraid he was dead, but I stayed by him, and presently, the battle swept on and we were left behind.

After a long time, my dear Master stirred a little, and opened his eyes when I licked his face, so, feeling very happy and joyful, I looked around for help. In the distance, I saw the stretcher men and I ran to them, calling for help as best I could. They knew me and were glad to follow where I led, for they said to each other, "Rice must be there" — and everybody loved him.

I heard them say it was "a bad job"; but they tied up his wounds, and carried him all the way back to the Hospital where he had taken me, and I followed very close, but alas! when they went inside they let the door slam quickly, and I, not expecting such a thing, was left outside alone; and, very sorrowfully, I sat down to wait.

VI

"Brave men are created by brave men."
Sir MAX AITKEN "Canada in Flanders."

I WAS perfectly determined to get inside that door no matter what happened, and I knew the best way was to make no noise but just to wait quietly, and sure enough, it was not so very long before the stretcher men themselves opened it to come out.

I was not going to lose my chance a second time, so I did not stop to speak to them but rushed in between their legs before they could stop me.

Once inside, I had no notion where to

find my dear Master, but I went smelling around the big entrance hall until at last I found the bearers had been up the stairs.

I bounded up in a perfect agony of anxiety, and just at the top, I met a woman in a white dress with the red mark on her sleeve. She looked at me in surprise and exclaimed in a kind voice, "Why, you dear doggie! How did you come to be here? What do you want?"

Then she took my head in her hands and looking into my eyes seemed to try her best to understand, while I looked at her earnestly and licked her hands. After a minute she said, "I don't think you had better stay here, little dog, come, come down with me' and as I did not move, she took hold of me, and tried to force me to go down.

I really could not stand that, so I just bared my teeth and growled gently to show her what I meant, and she must have understood, for she let me go, and said she would have to speak to the "Officer."

I did not wait to hear any more, you may be sure, but ran smelling and sniffling about under the doors which were all shut tight, until I came to one I was certain must be the right one, for I could tell that the bearers had been through it.

What with anxiety and the dust I had snuffled up my nose, I began to shiver, and sneezed several times, and though I tried to make as little noise as possible, somebody inside must have heard me, for the door opened a little crack, enough for me to get my nose in, and before the Person could think to stop me, I had pushed my way into the room.

What I saw there, I hate to think about, for it was my Master who was lying on the table bleeding and being bound and washed, so I just ran under the bed in the corner and lay quite still hoping they were too busy to bother me. After awhile, I could see from where I was lying that the Person who was working over my dear Master was the Surgeon who had taken care of me, and though I had never forgotten that he had said I was "only a dog," I believed he would understand that I must stay and watch.

When he seemed to have finished, I heard him say, "I believe I know this man, and if he is the one I think he is, we must make every possible effort to save him, for he is the kind England cannot now afford to lose."

When I heard him speak that way, I got up from my hiding place and went boldly to him and rubbed my head against his leg to make him notice me.

He looked down and said, "Hullo, little man, is it you?" and then to the others: "It is the man I meant, sure enough, for this is his dog, the one he saved. When he revives, it will probably give him heart to see his little comrade, so unless the dog gives you trouble, you may let him stay."

I just laid right down on the floor with a deep sigh when I heard this, I was so happy.

They were too busy to think any more about me just then, and when they had put my dear Master on the bed in the corner, I lay down beside him, and soon the table and all the horrid looking things were taken away, and we were left alone in peace, just my Master and me.

I raised myself up on my haunches so

that I could watch him, and wished as hard as I could that I might see him open his eyes. A long time passed and once in a while. a "nurse" (as I found they called the women in white dresses) would put her head in the door, and go quietly away again.

I had begun to despair, when all at once I saw my Master move his hands a little, and this made me so very-joyful I reached up and licked his face, very gently, and then, just imagine my feelings, when I saw the dear eyes open and heard a very faint voice say, "Army, — dear little laddie."

That was all, but it was enough, and the next time a nurse came to the door, I frisked silently around the room to show her that all was well.

Well, after this, my Master got better and we went to live in a great big room where there were a lot of other wounded men lying in the rows of beds, and everybody was my friend, and they never tried to send me away.

When he was feeling well enough. I used

to lie on the bed very close to him, but sometimes, he'd say, "Get down now, please, Army laddie, I carn't bear you now," and then I would lie under the bed, or sit beside it and watch him.

Those times when I lay beside him, he would talk to me of England, and of London, and how though he liked the country well enough, he loved the London streets even better.

"I used ter be a queer little bloke," he'd say, "I was carrier fer a big bookshop h'in Piccadilly an' I just got ter luv the books like they was 'umans. I luved the very smell uv 'em, an 'orfen I'd get a chawnce ter know sumthin' about the h'insides too.

"There was one chap by nayme uv Kiplin' now, 'e wrote such things, laddie, as stirred the 'eart, an' made me want ter fight fer England w'en the time came, as I'd never thought I would."

Sometimes he would repeat to me over and over words he had learned in those days. There was one verse he said so often, I got to know it well myself, and the men in the beds all round would ask him to say it again and again, until at last it got to be a regular thing when they were all dressed in the morning.

He would ask to be propped up on his pillows, and he would make me sit up in front of him, and then he'd say so proudly,

"If England was what England seems,

An' not the England of our dreams,

But only putty, brass, an' paint, —

'Ow quick we'd chuck 'er!

But she ain't!"

When he came to the last words, the men all over the room would shout them out just as loud as they could,— "But she ain't!" though some of the poor things

could hardly more than whisper, and then I was allowed to join in, "But she ain't!" and always gave one loud bark as a finish.

The first time we did it, I got so excited, I jumped off the bed and ran all up and down the room barking as loud as I could, but I never did it again, because the nurse my Master called "Sister," who was my special friend, explained to me that it made too much noise and excitement for all the sick People.

Things went on this way for some time until one morning I heard the Surgeon tell "Sister" that he was very much afraid Rice would not "pull through " after all, and that he had better be moved back to the private room and kept very quiet, and that perhaps the dog had better not be allowed in, though he'd leave that to her "judgment."

I didn't understand the meaning of that last word, and I searched all around her to see if I could find anything that looked like it, but she saw how worried I was and just patted me on the head and said, "You shall stay, little Army, for I know you'll be good, you dear little boy, when I've explained to you."

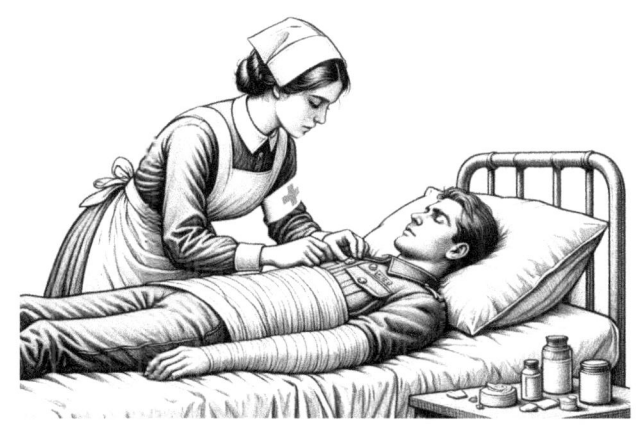

They soon moved him back to that quiet place and I could see that he was feeling very low in his mind, so I stayed quite close by to comfort him, and kept very, very quiet, hardly daring even to lick myself; for I didn't need to be told that he was very near to death.

VII

"An' last it come to me — not pride,
Nor yet conceit, but on the 'ole
(If such a term may be applied),
The makin's of a bloomin' soul."
— KIPLING.

THINGS went just about the same for several days, and you can imagine that I was happy to hear "Sister" say to the Surgeon, "Please, Sir, don't think of taking Army away, he is such a help, he watches just like a sensible human being, and if anything happened, I know he would come and find me, "so I was never troubled by anybody."

My dear Master suffered a great deal, but often, he seemed to find comfort in repeating some of the verses of the "Kiplin'" he loved. Sometimes it would be one thing and then another, but what he seemed to love most then was the part about "a bloomin' soul," for whenever he said that, he would smile and look so sort of satisfied; and then once in the night, he raised his head quite high and said almost in his old voice, "Judge of the Nations, spare us yet, Lest we forget— lest we forget!"

I knew quite well that he meant we must never forget the dreadful things those terrible big "Germans" had done to us, and I, for one, never- shall.

It must have been a great effort to him

Only A Dog

to say those words, for his head fell back on the pillow, and he never moved again all the rest of the night.

When morning came, I had gone fast asleep, and was waked up by hearing "Sister's" voice saying to someone: "It is all over at last"; and then I knew that he had not moved because he was dead, just like so many I had seen, only he looked quite as if he were at peace, and not horrible, like some of the others.

They tried to get me away, but I wouldn't move, and as I never interfered whatever they did, nor made a fuss when they put him in a box and carried it out, they let me follow. I watched them put him on the great big wagon, and waited while our regiment gathered together, and then I followed him, close behind, until they brought him here, and put him in this place they call a "grave."

Then the regiment stood at "'tention" and some of the men stood out from the others in a row, and fired guns, all together; and I knew they must be doing it because they loved him.

I had been dreadfully unhappy for I had thought that to be dead was the end, but there was a man in odd clothes there, "Chaplain" they called him, who read some nice comforting sounding words out of a big book. When I heard him say that a trumpet should sound, and the dead arise, I took heart again, and just determined to stay right here, until what he promised really happens. I should not like my dear good Master to wake and not find me waiting.

When they were going away, some of the soldiers I knew best tried to get me to go with them, but though I was quite willing to follow them as far as the gate, I would not go any farther, for I had learned only too well that if I went outside, and the gate shut tight behind me, I might never get in again.

One of them, the one I had loved best next to my Master, tried to take me in his arms and carry me out, and though I hated to seem ungrateful, I had to show him what I would do if he did not let me alone, so they saw they must let me have my own way, and went off.

I came back here and laid down on my Master's breast hoping that I might help him to keep warm, and I must say it seemed a very long dismal time before morning came again. When it did, I got up feeling very stiff and sore, and walked about the place, which I had heard them call a "cemetery," and I saw that it was almost full of "graves" just like my Master's, and that each one had a cross at the end of it.

While I was walking and looking about, I heard a whistle, sounding from the gate, and running towards it was delighted to see the same kind friend who had wanted to take me away. I showed him how happy I was to see him, and then he gave me some food he had thought to bring me. I ate it all up very quickly for it was a long time since anyone had thought to feed me, and when I had finished, I did everything I could to show my gratitude; but when he tried again to make me follow him, I just turned my back, and walked over here to this spot, where I have lived all the long weary time since.

He came again the next morning with more food, and every day in all this long time, he, or someone else, has done the same; and he brought one day my dear Master's coat and spread it for me to lie on, and it was Oh! such a comfort, to have something which seemed a part of him to keep me warm.

One day, after a long time, he came, and

brought a perfect stranger who wore some different looking things, and I heard them talking to each other about our regiment being ordered away. He said the new man must tell his regiment about me, and must "Promise faithful ter look after the pore little faithful chap, an' pass 'im on," if another regiment came.

Of course, I understood very well what they were talking about, and I could hardly bear to let my friend leave me, and I showed him so very plainly, but he had to go I know, for as my dear Master used to say, "A soldier 'as gotter obey h'orders, Army, no matter wot he thinks uv 'em."

The new man was very kind, and in time, I got to be quite fond of him and of the others in his regiment who came when he could not, but of course, they were never quite like the old friends I had lived with so long. They did the very best they could for me, and when the time came for them to go, they brought somebody from the new regiment and made them promise just the same as they had done, to look after me, and if they had to leave to turn me over to the new ones. When the time came that this happened, I heard them saying that it had become "a sacred charge handed down from the famous 42nd — s," and that nobody would ever dare to neglect a legacy of theirs. So for this reason, or because they were just kind, I never wanted for anything, and each regiment that came seemed almost kinder than the last.

One thing I do not understand is, why they all have the same name of "Tommy," and I often wish I could ask my dear Master to explain it to me, but of course I can't, and I just have to be patient about that, as about many other things.

Lately, the longing for my dear Master to wake up and let me be somewhere with him where we could be a little warmer and more comfortable has been almost more than I can bear, for I have felt so very, very tired, and would not have touched the food the Tommies brought me if they hadn't seemed so very disappointed.

Tonight, the latest Tommy was particularly kind, and I did hope his feelings wouldn't be hurt, but I just couldn't eat, nor even swallow a drop of water.

He sat by me a long time, and it was very comforting to feel his warm hand gently smoothing me, and to hear his kind voice saying, "Pore little Army, pore little chap, it's almost finished, you won't 'ave ter wait much longer."

Then I felt something hot and wet drop on my head and I knew he was crying; a luxury I have often wished I might indulge in, for it always seems to be such a comfort to People. But I never could, though I've tried often.

I had heard the bugle sounding and I knew he ought to go, but he waited and waited, and fidgeted a bit, but at last said with a sigh, "I do 'ate ter leave yer, boy, but I must, so good-bye little faithful one, an' w'en my time comes, may I 'ave done 'arf as well."

He went away then, and feeling very desolate, I tried to lift my head a little to look around me. It was still light, and it looked to me very beautiful, for the apple-trees in the cemetery, which they had made in an orchard, were in full bloom, and I had heard my friends say that "Spring" had come.

It seems very wonderful to me that the trees, so dead all Winter, should be covered now with these lovely flowers, which I love to have fall over me and my dear Master, and I cannot help hoping it means that it is nearly time for him to wake. He has slept so long.

It is strangely cold just now, and is growing very dark... I wish that kind Tommy could have stayed... It is so very hard to be alone tonight; I wonder why? ... I never minded it before.

Only A Dog

Dear, dear Master! If you would only come! Even your dear coat does not warm me any more! …. So tired — so — very — tired.

AFTER

"Be thou faithful unto death, and I will give thee a crown of life."

— REVELATION ii., 10.

THE next morning, "The Latest Tommy" asked to speak to his nearest "Non Com.," and what he said so puzzled that man, he was for a moment speechless. Then, scratching his head reflectively he answered, "Well, I can't say, I'm sure; there's nobody but the Colonel himself could give the order. If I could get the message up to him now, through all the others, he's such a good sort, he might say to put it through. Anyhow, Tommy, me boy, we can but try."

The message was evidently one which worked its way, for by midday, "The Latest Tommy" was sent for by the great man himself.

Very nervous, not feeling at all sure how his request might be taken, he was ushered into the Colonel's own private den and found him sitting at a table absorbed in writing. With feet which seemed to him to take up all the room, and hands which would not keep still, "Tommy" stood whirling his cap round and round in a perfect agony, until he suddenly became aware of a stern voice, saying: "Stop twirling that cap, my man, and answer me. You are Private S. — ? and you made a singular request of your Non Com. this morning, — am I right?"

"Ye — yes — Sir," stammered Tommy.

"Well, speak up, I'm very busy, but I'm also interested, what is it?"

"It... it's about the little dog 'Army,' Sir, wot you must 'ave 'eard uv, Sir. The little faithful fellow's laid on his Master's grave all winter long, an' now, this mornin', 'e's dead. Mebbe yer 'aven't rightly 'eard the story, Sir, 'ow Rice in the 42nd — s crept out into No Man's Land an' brought the little beggar 'ome in the face uv the h'enemy's fire, an' 'ow 'e an' the doctor mended 'im w'ere they devils 'ad shot 'im, an' 'ow 'e stuck tight ter Rice allus, an' couldn' by no manner nor means be forced ter leave 'is grave w'en Rice died, Sir, an' 'ow the Reg'ment ᶠed 'im 'an' looked arfter 'im, an' guv 'im ter the next, an' the next, h'until 'e cum down ter us, Sir.

"Larst night, I feared 'e was a dyin', an' h'it mos' broke me 'eart ter leave 'im alone; an' now, Sir, wot we wants is, ter pay 'im some sort uv 'onor, Sir, like wot 'is own Reg'ment would 'a done. Ef yer please, Sir, ef yer cud let the Reg'ment go out, as many as cud, an' let us 'ave the bugle call; us men 'd all thank yer, Sir, fer lettin' alone luvin' the little chap, Sir, we don't none uv us want the 42nd — s ter think we've failed 'em."

As he ended his breathless little speech, "The Latest Tommy" was not ashamed openly to wipe his eyes.

The Colonel also seemed to find something of unusual interest on his desk, but at last he looked up and said, "I'm glad to hear the story, S., and I will give orders that it may be done as you and the others wish. Of course, it will have to be about sunset, when our friend Fritz over there generally gives us a rest.'

Saluting with a fervor he had never experienced before, The Latest Tommy hurried away, and late that afternoon, for some time before sunset, men in full accoutrements might have been seen in little groups finding their way back to the cemetery behind the town.

There, in the beautiful field of the dead under the blossoming apple-trees, a full company gathered and watched "The Latest Tommy" and another, as they wrapped the little body in the Master's cloak and laid it carefully in the small grave made as close as possible to the big one. Then, when the spade had done its work with the very same sound we all know so well, the loud sharp command of "Shun"! was heard, and the company stood rigid in honor of the little faithful soldier, until a bugle, clear and sweet, sounded the "Retreat." The call of the dying Day to the vanished Sun...

By twos and threes, the men silently melted away, until "The Latest Tommy" found himself alone, as he smoothed the grave and tidied up the ground around it. When all was finished to his satisfaction, he rested on his spade, and said with a deep sigh, "I'll miss the little beggar, though I'm glad 'is sufferin' 's over.

"I wonder now, I do... 'Ere's all these chaps lyin' 'ere dead, they guv their lives cos they knew good 'ol Hengland needed 'em; an' Army 'ere, 'e guv 'is cos 'e thought 'is friend needed 'im.... All uv 'em faithful 'til death..."

Silent and thoughtful, he stood under the darkening sky, looking up at the stars as they twinkled one by one out of the blue… Then, lifting his cap reverently, he said slowly… "I wonder, I do… but Gawd… He knows."

www.ingramcontent.com/pod-product-compliance
Lightning Source LLC
Chambersburg PA
CBHW052103070526
44584CB00017B/2321